St. John's Rose Slumber

David Need

Spuyten Duyvil
New York City

Selections from this manuscript have appeared in Hambone, Minor Americans (1) and on the Philly Fan Site and quarrtsiluni websites.

COVER IMAGE: Valentin de Boulogne, French, 1591-1632: *St. John the Evangelist*, c. 1622-1623; oil on canvas. canvas: 38 5/16 × 52 15/16 in. (97.3 × 134.5 cm), frame: 47 3/8 × 61 7/8 in. (120.3 × 157.2 cm). Ackland Art Museum, University of North Carolina at Chapel Hill. The William A. Whitaker Foundation Art Fund, 63.4.1

© 2019 David Need
ISBN 978-1-949966-51-0

Library of Congress Cataloging-in-Publication Data

Names: Need, David, author.
Title: St. John's rose slumber / David Need.
Description: New York City : Spuyten Duyvil, [2019]
Identifiers: LCCN 2019026157 | ISBN 9781949966510 (paperback)
Subjects: LCSH: John, the Apostle, Saint--Poetry.
Classification: LCC PS3614.E27 A6 2019 | DDC 811/.6--dc23
LC record available at https://lccn.loc.gov/2019026157

Alongside the Gospel of John not as exegesis or act of
devotion skirts but as wander, as one wanders with a book
that is read, or as bookplates to the chapters a child would
recall. Alongside the shore of, woven in and out.

A look out the window of the church across landscape
otherwise seen from cars, and *in dialogue*
as is necessary in this doubled world.

Contents

St. John's Rose Slumber

Part One: Parables

I	Diagram Stray	3
II	Wedding Songs	7
III	Tabernacles at Night	11
IV	Twilight Well	13
V	Bethesda	16
VI	A Scent of Loaves	17
VII	Folded Tents	21
VIII	Olivestones	23
IX	Where Blinding Pools	26
X	Climb Up Some Other Way	30
XI	Bethany	33
XII	In Fields of Fallen Wheat	35

Part Two: The Last Supper

XIII	Footwashing	41
XIV	A Mansion on a Hill	44
XV	Plumbline	47
XVI	A Little While	50
XVII	Prayers	54

Part Three: Crucifix & Resurrection

XVIII	Death's Trials	61
XIX	Cross	
	Eyes	68
	Stations or (Saturday Afternoon to Wonderland)	72
	Wrapped Shrouds	75
XX	Touch My Side	79

Part Four: Aftermath

XXI	Beside the Sea	85

PART ONE:
PARABLES

Chapter I:
Diagram Stray

I

Inside   inside was is to be
as inside is thinks was
was
become as

***

all relations of is are beautiful as
angles

the threads of my fingers
    are the threads of my words
where birds arc
    so too the traces I furrow thick

what can be said is not meaning but justified.

On a different morning, I was considering caring.
It was a habit, a way to be disposed among stores.
Always interested in arrangement I was considering
this profile or that? This street or that?
It is easy enough to transpose the problem
into a secondary,
but one remains haunted.

In this wise I watched a pigeon walk unsteadily under the wheels of a truck.

Right here all that descending had happened long ago.

"Lamb Chops", the distant girl used to call
       whenever I went to Cleveland front yard,
distant, pinafores and waving, vanishing
       "Lamb Chops"—

"In the Beginning was the Word" it said,
wood word was aster

*

He was washing by Heidegger's swamp in the reeds
A black man, bent over, against bright green yellow
sun startled water   a different black reflection
the eyes scattering   heron and blackbirds

II

And so it was:
        is death for me;
silence twice
        a spanse —

what other notation
        but love? You'd go
beneath the curtain.
        I'd say: we're there.

What's one more blanket?
        Don't ask who I am.
The stars resist ambition —

all shepherds know
        the soft sands,
the way to water.

III

Oh the sign, oh the sign is not...

the long hunger to have
        and the broken rib: a sparrow;
the senses are

moist figs,
        a suspended
chance: manifold and threaded

elsewise into bracken.

Chapter II:
Wedding Songs

I

Desire and argument, Joe talks about these... how argument sharpens desire
        acts as a stage of amplification.
The Bible comes out when explanation gets over-labored —
        perhaps we meant the way the Gospels are

fire, simply fire, to touch,
        to be consumed,   the
rhythms of hummingbirds and
        thrush,   where

word became astra   (sigil over
        balconies)
becomes condensed aster petals,

discs of Michael grey
        sewn into weddings
and shirtcloth gorse.

II

No one can escape longing:
        plunge into the river,
and get swept to the sea.

Only the receding bank
        tells you different:
what's gone
    is direction.

III   The Festal

Scaffold scars of the sky in
      muddy paths —

the scaffolds became stars,
      effort-sent pillars
& arms thrown wide —

the scaffolded script
      in constant telling
was stars, the meadow
      beneath,

script thread slipped
      into constellated arras
w/butterflies.

IV

This is what it means to be a rose
       — he was pointing to a window,
the sill and split,
       the scaffolding wine pulsed

out 'neath the pressing seal —
       symbol's twice.
I was land inside, she was split where I was tree.
       It was brocade, my ear

A root. He rides the sun of my eyes,
       the dapples and falls,
the folded napkin and winter,

as if I were a hand
       he could offer —
broken in two.

Chapter III
Tabernacles at Night

I

Nicotine-stained windows as saint's blood,
 a carapace ash   inside silent hallway mirrors,
cards dealt still on candle-lit table bistro,
brown mud alley's extrusions of brown mud & donkeys—

at the convention center a more startling boat show
where the image has been, erased,
dig farther down than the stone tile, than the grubs, than frayed
not-light (the dazzling) because even stores

may be justified; what lifts a man is already lifting,
what lifts the clouds,   what tangles of gorse, quince, and strawgrass
as this spring's under sky   its window-sill   its looking—

to say this much is to say too much
& shush,
its hard not to cross over that line
& grace's eyes are closed

as spring.

II

At time's fold: the already present
        that is knot — past whose future manifests into being as —
what still point is that "Be Here Now?"
        was dreamt, though all

solutions are endless.
        Becoming matters only as identity's same,
but not when sensed;   instead is withers,
        fruit as burgeon: a splitting.

That twice here
        equals actual death
or better, unsummed,

since (already already already
        only this happened
and was.

Chapter IV:
Twilight Well

I

Infinite on   the impossible task
    as scented sparrows across the chalk grass
the wind folds a season   beside a well
    as pocket of sun —   Drink what's below

drink what's below that.   Ladle your hand slip
    your hand put into the sun
or lap the surface black accordion heart
    as lost form's music   as the between

desire opens   my instrument also of love
    this taste   not desire's endless as
that meeting the vine's border

all tapestry and bread
    limits of skin and tongue
that furrow.

II

The reading: a city can be moved
      but not a well.

So then   buildings disappear in a flurry of wings?
     a migration   or, slipped into the sky as they so often
threaten?   leavened Manhattan learward a listing orphan ship —

     some maps are like a steady wind that force
prophecy upon us,   the bustle
     of words (like lithographic acid) cuts the tree,
wears the apple to limestone wash   blind orioles sing
     the orphic solution   so do we more slowly:

imagined immigrant
     she stood by the clothesline   at the bottom of the airshaft
marked the solstice shadow

fish darted in the air.

III

Scarf'd face & star's scaffold
    beside the cistern's steps —

that fairy tales named: rose red and the white,
that doubled said: maid talking to man,
that doubled said: made song,
that doubled said: she slept wake,
    had passed into meadows.

She said, "Become rose red, the whiter follows
    as if bound, was sister's friend,
as thought follows sound, so the angel stoops
    towards death;
be split into,
be the darker love   the earthen sunset mews
    whose spelling secret fashions walls
divide."

Only the cracked vessel leaks
    the whiter pure remember,
seeps into the fields,

the more immediate body listens.

Chapter V
Bethesda

In any text there
                is the closet door
      and the unsatisfied
& clumsy

& then there are the days of panic

as a second and a third voice begin the clamor

one lifted out of the water still cannot breathe
        and the river sparkles with salmon

here and there along the throng's passage
        there are doorways

where one might step aside
        into brief seasons of some silence

see, through the archway there, Provence
      or an atrial moss   in clay blues

a mirage of healing: the bone needs   an auger
      before it can be   a flute

the spaces between weedings are not the same as growth
      Marat›s fingers almost touch   our asphalt monument to solutions

but do not.

Chapter VI:
A Scent of Loaves

Feast here earth's beings
    on this hand, in this bowl
the left curled towards the sun (finger'd rain)
    or belly fat grilled tan
the buttery smooth   toll ghosts beside the back door
    this fine thin bone
and the child terrors and small sparrows
    the pincers and sudden dropped plates
and the crawling fear   and the right hand
    in a blue bowl   take that too
as fishes.

By the red rock mosque on the tiled sand
by the red rock that climbed out of the flood
beside the red rock and the blue sky
    under the stars   under the trees   under the shadows
beneath the season's clouds   and the swallows
amidst sparrows   on the stone floor.

***

She bared one arm
she bared the other
she took the bright cleaver
she cut off the left
she held it in the air.

This is the branch, the first stanza, the threshold
    shoulder   eat it to cross   my look
into the room   only you could imagine

see? I grind the fingers to breadcrumbs   bring the birds too

from this point on   its all interpretation.

*

She stretched out her left foot
she stretched out her right
she took the bright cleaver
she cut them both off
she put them in a box
she held it in the air.

This is the ark   you imagined   the room upstairs
    I throw them into the room
Only when a dream is digested   does it become a suitable day
    I would have you look out the windows.

She took off her clothes
she took the bright cleaver
she cut off her skin
she shook it out   in the air.

This is the next veil   the gauze on the windows   the breath
    in the room   everything between us   is skin
I suggest we make it a table   set the places.

The joint between one word and the next flaps like a knee.

***

She took the bright cleaver
she cut out her liver
she laid it in a bowl.

She cut out her stomach
she laid it in a bowl

she cut out her spleen
she laid it in a bowl

she cut out her intestines
she laid them steaming among these

she cut out her eyes
she cut out her tongue

she cracked open her ribs
she laid out her lungs

she broke open her skull
she laid out her brains

she cut out her heart
and threw it in the air.

Eat my liver you
eat my bowels

eat my spleen with salt
and the stomach parch

the brains with spinach
and lung stew

make small slices in my heart
drain the blood
mix with grapes and juice and thyme.

Hey all you   eat!
Hey all you   eat!

I am trying to show you   the only way out
the present   is a gift   not what's immediate

but a room   you can enter

that I've never seen.

***

[One-Mother-Low-Down said this
lapsed mountain desperate
happening.

[If it's a room it's a room through flesh.
That is: sitting in a room where the air is flesh
or moving through flesh is to enter into a surface
call it water it is substance being no space before our
eyes beautiful eyes
because what is beauty but a ferry ticket and
I could call it grass it'd be or windows or sea surface
I could say poor crowd spectacle I could say flensed or
flexed room which makes you think of a light bulb
how else angled shadows?
The diagram on the floor specifies the momentary shapes
we must observe we move against
like tattoos.]

Chapter VII
Folded Tents

I

A shoe floats in the bathtub
which is already to have become separated
not as knuckle   or barnacle tapestry   because the hinge
makes room   from sparse throat.

If this was going on in the basement it was
nevertheless not obvious from the kitchen where the mother
moved among copper-toned pans   a brown still-life
with toaster   more still than wallpaper.

Hard to discuss the sun what I am hearing from the sun.

Instead the particular angle of her look a rock a large rock
rolled against the French windows

the measured steps of depression
     as the body›s loyalty
             to the less articulate
certainties,

thoughts like roses nevertheless acid

all blues as entrance to the more splendid garden

a book open by the sundial spilling winter
     the words like birch branches   spattering

threads in and among the grass.

II

The foil-wrapped saint is barely enough for the sky's pain
    the hysterical sad walls   mad with moan:
room after room   abandoned bibles   bedclothes
    something almost Christian about the absence
in old men's eyes   something downright Christian about the paint
    such harbors of humbleness   so many seals.

It was, after all, possible only to suggest such suffering
    it was a matter of pigments, a kind of selection
which stones to place over which joints   and what to use
    to weigh down the belly.
We were, after all,   hoping to make an anchor   since we would
    rather fly away;   we want an open sky   a passing
that leaves no profile   to plummet   but we have
    hands   pliant fingers   that can distinguish seeds.

If you pour enough of this wash over the surface its like you were drunk.

Here's another bucket.

Winter is just the other side of kindled light

Chapter VIII
Olivestones

I

Memory catches the clothes   torn free from the wash line
    in a wind of olives   and alabaster

because we are buffeted by earlier habits
because the past has several aspects.

The seasons come in such disarray
    cast between statues and mercy;

Drawn idly   the bison gather the years
    of solutions   but the light in their faces
it's difficult to say.

This slippage among mediums and styles   cannot be erased
    by stones   love marks us all with chalks
perhaps the light breaks out this way

in a wind of olives   and alabaster

but is not recovered.

II

Rabia would not marry
    as her love of God made her
a useless wife, distracted at the window
    always throwing out a hand.

It was in this way that she arranged
    sin differently,
a horizon not marked by light
    but hollows.

III

Mercy's ear is among crickets —
    the lilting special fields distract
empty houses grave   grass returns between
    the floorboards.   This is the way

mercy lasts   waits longer.   Clouds pass —
    fiddling wind strap slap —

Intoxicated knot   as mercy's gnarl
    breath›s evidence   proves the greater tolerant
space

your stones could cover

the asphalt sky
    all patterned.

Chapter IX
Where Blinding Pools

I

He said: I will separate my voice a moment:

How much I am stretched
      across by the
cycles of wooing —
      impossible ruptures —

I've made a dish of myself
      after all father

What came before this uprooting want
      this become scaffold
before body became a shadowed pond
      space of sky?

What shows through?
      the grass? patches
of memory;
      where the sun fell?

Later that afternoon
      desire again takes my hand
and leads me   towards boats
      the day settles into a piano
thus episodic fenced horizons.
      Everything civil   is possible

but I am not so
      easy.

Even as I write this   she was leaving by a different
        door

that is to say,
        the day was woven.

***

Having cut things this way
        and laid them out that

he thought, "fence or tapestry?
        trellis or veil?

Everything is   twice   mercy at least.

II

He bent over the blind man his holly pail
        he was dipping his hand
he was saying the blind man
who said "yes long ago I broke
I see there was no other choice
the prism of desire had bent the world
but it was my thigh that had the code

ripping my eyes out making a meal of them
        nothing changed

I had fallen into the long avenue of imagining
        into the aspens and silent hotels;
what had become shadow
        what color is
you say also light too   that were fenced
        as   I am married to the depths.

Wound woos.   I can say I see
        but words divide   not seeing
but slumbering lids closed as braised light filters

even you."

III

A man lay listening his eyes dyed in color
      following the red girl
deeper into the painted fixtures;
      sparrows flitted among the icon rafters

the sky sunk in grey apartments;
      the absent world murmured prices
as fugue chant   slanted light
      was unheard

but its results; the words broken into
      window flowers; guttering fragments
of shadows as alert

the birds chittering,
      as blossom; the stone's still
warmth.

Chapter X
Climb Up Some Other Way

I

She had been coming in and out the upstairs window
I'd have said it was about glass houses,
but the window was unlocked   anyway the sun came across

the sill   as she moves about upstairs, I wonder
why am I still here, years later   on this rug
the shadows of leaves make a deeper heart
a play of shadows and light   I imagine my fingers
doing something as beautiful.   Serif and curl
possible fences or steep   but the word
is not the sun.   The sun moves where the image does not

on the floor a body or a lake   the shadow of a body
in a poem   I make images after this   all the while
she is coming in and out the window upstairs
she steps over the leaky stain on the floor

she steps past where the roof leaks
she crosses to the bureau   does something else in the attic

then she's gone again
and clouds of dust and sun.

II

Be leave as breath does
     where vine splits rock in
asters' clustered   skirts
     spelled rhyming;

rings out the distant shatters.
     Cloud vicarage where valleyed, drops
away, as the nixed breath shelters
     even still

wined weathers.
     Be leave as falls the day
cascade in splashes

stone, scaffold sheep
     surround
left dreaming after.

III

Are there any other ways to read she asks?
I wish I could listen the way a house does.
He flexed his arm.   Metaphors are like sinews.
They produce a pull. It is never in a straight line.
Muscles fibers are arranged in a torus.
Calculus is not better for this.
There is room   somewhere over here.

Chapter XI
Bethany

I

Because touch

beneath which open rooms   countless blooms distill

realms: invisible hands trace   sparrow wings
      among the pulse-veils   the pleurisy
tasted

blossoming wounds

as spit.

See this: the kingdom death discloses
    no ground not vanishing
all about as startled   air
    in which this   passed image

was.

II

It was   gravestones among sisters
     arising after —   one rushed
towards the coffin

bright skirted & brunette   as wood
     one stone blond still
in blue dress   & an osprey alit where her arm

he had upspilled the lid   eyes open
had crawled back the countless grass too many lids

lay slumbering

from which the stars gathered
as molten gold
and fell a disc   struck

precise this bridge;

as if exhaled
a stunned sparrow springs
from the opened hand

from no   wear
a distance struck

and bent to tear   -stain
warbled

this uneven   ground.

Chapter XII
In Fields of Fallen Wheat

I

What solution is fire?

(the roof leaks
        partly out of myth

a water-stained book is special as bled
    on spider-plant sill)

— No,
    because words are water
        surface ponds of eyes
as risen serif
    the buildings blazen
the otherwise sky
    discursive.

In the after of rain
    reflection sky
like new cotton
    falls behind the eyes
arras;

to be written
        the loss   salves.

II

I was again, in the field, accepted
as thoroughly   as the grass is,
the way what lights me knots
day and night,   a piece of the veil
threaded into birch trees,   the distant city
and my arm, the north and ocean
particular gulls, a spring sun —

that I would no more be outlawed
that she would no more have the trees rebuke
that the sea was not set
that thrown out was over
forever she said   we will not again say this
bitter is marriage
our back not turned
delights.

III

    If I'd advice it'd be:
        go against your best
    talent so's you come back
        the other side.

    Then desire in breath
        takes what root would
    have it; then the unseen imagined
        fire

    becomes seasonal.
        Because the hand is more
    easily taught   friendship

    across the grain
        made possible by falling
    both.

IV

Against the grain: except that an ear,
      here, in the field — poppies in red August cloud;
shame's blanketing dawn
      is juggled into a puzzle; this way

the winnowing after solution;
      before solution, the ground ponds deep;
nothing lies between,
      so no heart.

Whether by logic's trace or bloom perceived.
      the move askance —
tracks amidst the fallen wheat
      and still the ear.

Heart's angling arrow
o'er reason's fence.

Part Two:
The Last Supper

Part Two:
The Last Supper

Chapter XIII
Footwashing

I

Somehow I had ended up next to Mary;
she was sitting on the porch it was like a pier hanging over the driveway
someone close was talking about this Buddhist chant:
nam myo ringge kyo   'sposed to bring gold
and someone else had been saying about
meeting other very high people over California
in astral ships;   they were captains.
I was listening for clues   but none of this seemed promising.
I knew it was hopeless it was just habit now   the trail cold
had been closed   there had been very definite dreams about this:
her bowl had broken
it was hard to have a house with many rooms
someone says "hi David"
do you say, "excuse me I am in the kitchen right now?"
its seems apparent
gauzey walls of midnight
your floor plan doesn't match.
It's like working at a splinter in the mirror
you have to think "Left. Left, no her left"
and then there are places that don't seem to have doors
then you have to resort to myth
start looking around on the ground.

Anyway Mary she had whole sequences that were only dimly apparent
the night seemed to be her
there was some confusion over drinks
the people around her were mean and I got stuck talking to them
maybe its okay to say negative things I don't
I was perhaps confused   about the exit point
It had happened before
It wasn't really that much of a problem.

II

What divides me from the sheets of day that parse before me
that I am somehow serial as blink,
that sandaled moon makes such a yawning of

all skim this edge of body.
You cannot drown in color
which removes a part of light to see
a softer reminder's
pull.

A broken wheel that all divides reveal
does not resist to say
dialogue's the art   the birch
that splits   its seeds.

III

What happened was that the body is not so transparent as thought and
        needed washing
wash-lines sagged; water wicked in the wind, sliding between colors
damp skin, knob-finger splayed brooch,   stops the throat;
in these terms, the voice shifts to an argument in prose; authority is
        referred to
as if he were not in the room   could be flame;   spatial tone
        gives way to
the production of urgency; this this clatters the tongue
which should be hand, slapping the sponge, slapping the water spilling
laps over the bowl   the floor glistens   water drops through
        everything
gravestone as plumbline   underlime   stone lids
                                                            a taste of fruit.

Chapter XIV
A Mansion on the Hill

I

It had started to unravel
this business of stories relating to stories
this business of codes;

at the dinner last night it was as if I had been
at a different table
to the left of where we sat;

I was translating well enough
to sustain the lie;
it was hard to believe anyone

anyone could fail to notice.   It was the high tone of it
I was unwilling to say more than "please"
there were so many possible rooms, and

all of them were apart.

II

A radio in the other room played Elvis Costello's
"Waiting for the End of the World."

It was a full moon
we were on our way to the green woman's house
there was supposed to be a party
I'd shoplifted some lamb earlier in the day
Amy suddenly thought we were all vampires and ran back to the dorm.

On the apartment complex lawn Russell passed out the lamb
all that catholic shit
the raw juice ran in his beard
at least we knew the lines to the Rocky Horror Picture Show
some other ghost dance, about to become "America's Most Wanted"
out of what suburban basements and ping pong hours?

Mornings falling through cascades of designer shoes
searching through paisley shirts for a well
only bad roles and worse   strangled music
Zappa and Rungren   fetish solutions made of Beethoven
just human have to move after a little bit not so strong
what're the options tonight among worse Shoney's buffet
move put the radio on pick up "operation" or shoeboxes
full of baseball cards.

Because the heart will always need to take action.

III   *Mirabilia*

Doubled houses   steps to the attic;
but it was the body   the body   opened out like a room
it was   a place for some memory   like a stove   or
where she'd been   the coiled rug   was that inside the body too?
that ceiling?   or is it in words   in loops of words?
like fleck beak   or drop the sea
as electrical densities?   as salt passages?
How is the past inflected this time   that cathedral glass was spent breaking?
spelled room as thigh   this window to birds.

Chapter XV
Plumbline

I

"You don't understand," he was saying
        "God's problem with gay sex —
he requires a blood sacrifice
        marriage sheets split virgin red."

Chapel steps and surrounding trees suitably hushed,
        a usual scattering of birds,
cars pulling in and out. It all seems modern,
        timeless. Lenten Cardinals flirt through quince.

Someone must have explained it to him this way.
        A long chain of some bodies.
a confusion of furnishings:

even in contracts, a marriage precedes
        atonement; otherwise
the table   was never ruined.

II

I don't mean to sound bored about this; I should have spoken up about
AIDS,
        that blood passes to blood across wounds
as more ardent sacrifice; he would have pointed to a different chapter;
after all
        he wasn't making sense.   Hidden statues hung in misery as
awful tapestry

the constant violence. What is beautiful in yellow-grey marble is the body
        shouting back it could be flowers, even twisted around
the cross its lifted windows its barns the fields from a car
        small telephone-wire dreams in the rapid silence.

As if sacrifice were the way to wed what's split to the groin,
        or Hegel's dialectic — it's the same dice
scattered on middle ground, a logic of answers weaves

the confessional grill between; what has come apart spills in the air
        in bursts, drifts over the corn fields
falls.

III

What is true but gravity love? A branch that runs its angles,
    rises undecided,   between water and sun,
and slithers like a river to leaf   because we are all pulled
    by cross tides,   and groan the season   cloudswept.

A vine twines around a lattice stone   around other wood
    occasional grapes cluster   where sunlight dances
                                          a chance avenue
where colors more brightly gather   skirts and feathers of peeling
                                                  bells.
    Across the street a girl turns profile

lacing up looks into aster could-be   armpit hollows like summer
                                              shadows
    wed an afternoon shower;   come and see.
Cat mint takes over a garden   lower gowns into a well.

And, well,   say nay the decider   that like you was overgrown
    and meant sorrow.   Come and see!
Come and see!

Chapter XVI
A Little While

I

It's a way of speaking   to say into the four directions
various angels of air
like fingering trumpet scales —   as East (four fingers): the window
and South (two): always a sunnier clime   and so on
running fingers through chimes of air   sealing the eye as

sparrow hiding in holly as it rains

something precise   a way back to water
world thrown down like a coin as purchase   scant purchase.

A reiteration of quadrants and avenues and parsed sentences
by which de sign sorts.

(She said, you cannot enter the house that way;
you have to somehow lift the crossroads up like a scaffold
like a ladder   up to the attic
or the bedroom on the roof
you have to climb up onto it

you have to curl your body until it is like a doorknob
until it is curled around the center where
the avenues cross
which is not the present
which is not sublime
which is not between

gives way
like a secret panel
a sudden leak
as a month's period begins
slippage under the foot of a moon.)

Directions like these only work in dreams;
they are otherwise provocation.

II

Can you reach into him & find what you love?
It's the only question
as confidence I no longer ask.

Among the shelves perhaps   daffodils in the rain
an arrangements of words   that satisfies —
is it the same?

Precise morning light will tell the difference.

There are a number of things I desire;
they are piled at the door.

This business of who is in whom and what is the brushwork of the sun —
a steady application of color in specters to make region field.
The body's boundary is only half skin;
the other half is window and smoke.

What is felt is arm   even when it lingers at the end of the street.

To be scattered is not hard;
sex is simply the most emphatic rupture;
for days after there is a sorting out —
when we were young it was model planes
the collection of belongings that begins each day.

At least images make this easier
and profiles.

Mirrors wrinkle the surfaces like fingers on a harp;
some parts are not recovered.

She left this more elaborate quilt of brambles and lilac
so that we too would have to pick our way.

III

You ask me if my heart is true since riddled by dreams of a dark,
        a lady and her sister, the following light,
and so crooked in this not quite whole some   desiring face
        fastened to appear, drunk   up a straw

— this confusion of habitude often becomes me
        whether I was you, or had already left,
the opposite bank flashes in sunlit   companion;
        I touch the earth, changing hands   authentic dolphins

clear their skulls   into and among flashing seams;
        this is the way a good coat   is made
fold the cloth   dart the hand   to catch the wave's shovel;

just off port   the elements change banks again,
        hourglass word turns to stone   then softens
as appearance blooms.

Chapter XVII
Prayers

I

this porch among fallen winters
space of my hand
on your shoulder

****

a secret room behind the books
your daughter's footsteps
on stairs to the basement

****

body becomes field
and so can answer sun, "asters"
and so wait

****

fire
no longer secret
is autumn
my father's diagram

****

a priest lazy in a field
careless
mistakes ideas
for flowers

****

oh, rose
split
makes possible
the hidden skies

****

face, first of all, prow
filled with water
your cupped hands

****

what moves in them
but fallen winters
your shoulder ahead

****

a translation to kiss
as I am shadows
her daughter

****

and so founded

****

so you also
speak stones across the river
spark

****

a path back
inside myself
lifts dream

****

skirt lifted
her feet descend
a last ridge

****

ocean rose
blueblack in her hair
and iris

****

eyes shut lips shut
ears shut   the shuttered doors
of icons

****

a candle guttered
a city became shepherd
these for you

****

majesty

****

in star folds

****

in your pocket.

Part Three:
Crucifix & Resurrection

II

A dream:
long pebbly beach like dove brown
boats pulled up on the shore & ancestor fisherman sling nets
under Van Gogh or Wyeth reference tide scramble to a tower.
A look sweeps north along the break to the horizon then inland.
We follow looks I follow the look around the tower
a festival wedding in stated cordials a fence of tables
her father's a big man you can tell a big man power
but what's all that?
A dance spirals out hand-to-hand flower girl white glove
he's in the center, slouch hat, piper black coat
looks down long nose
death majestic coattails swirling
that's her father
we keep dancing
hand-to-hand.

Chapter XVIII
Death's Trials

I

Solution as fisherman   for me something Wyeth
    but that'll disappear
and the castle on the flinty Maine shore   not quite
    as a camera pans around it   wave swept
white boats pulled onto the pebbly sea shoal   a
    The camera pulls around, voice over saying
"one thing our family does not know how to do is funera
    because a stone beach   because it was left

counts need things   to say   because th
    listening.

He's so slouch hat so majestic so swirl so black coat mafia
    surrounded by a circling   (something British,
                                        festal la

wicked truth in each vine.

It ends   makes festive   sound.

III

I am not a slip-knife wind that finds a middle
        word or distance — that is just the truth
all things carry
        of an other's interior.

The East that I shape in my hands is lent
        shelters of white oaks;
        a range between skylights
and fairytales begin to resonate what hunger
        clears.   Among the answers

too many recent dead
        to tend

instead open
        eyes & shattered flower literals

under an awn sky.

IV

Not of this world
    which sense finds between
the fingers of a rose-last
    thorn-spark separate.

As no kingdom
    willed who falls
rain-curtain
    across

the lost, the lost among them.

******

Did his eyes reflect dolphins
    or receded chambers glimpsed
black-currant   river wharf
    did depths dream?

Among the reports   not one word
    suggests
close glances;   perhaps abstract
    is not sighted

but clothes. Sealed eyes
    under lip's hand
saw what?

Your remembering
    is all that
        calls.

V The Crowd

I

He say, "You trying to fly out of the body boy
    I'm going to fix that, me,"
hits me on the side of the neck whack
    bones groan but break open and take
the weight back.
    "Okay, I'll try to hold all this
here down here,
    so it pulls something to it."

"See, its only when the weight of the Logos
    'your best dream you'
falls
    its only when the most beautiful thing falls

    its only then
    it finds its form
    gets married
    and things get interesting.

"I am saying you dream the best dream you
    fly all that power you feel
    all that sky in you
    that electric guitar
    that big thing that
    cloud
into weight
    & world starts to circulate & breath."

II

'nuther guy says, "This boy?" takes the bird someone give him
        and throw it over his shoulder into the house says,
"more water."
First guy says, "exactly, that's what I am talking,"

and then the lover-hero starts talking about this lady
she visits him at night gathers up over his bed.
He knows he's dreaming feels her
and he says, "all this time it was just the light touch
of some great power
falling."

He says "I dreamed she was tied up in a garden,
I wanted to save her, but the first step
was to be a kid again in a nomad camp
someplace Himalaya
among some kind of shamans
keeping the fires going,
and only after that could I start back
with my captain whose armor
whose armor was a shout of red."

They all smile hard not to love a lover-hero
"you go boy" they say "you go love the night
when autumn is thickest
when what's announced
becomes word."

"When August skies turn their spears
back towards the earth
all the silver rains down
it rains hammers
and stars fall
back to become trees again
and next years flowers."

"And one time I was on a hill
and all the stars gathered into one star
and that star fell
it fell right into my hand
was a disc like St. Michael's medallion
like Michaelmass asters
like a mudra seal pressing my hand
compassionate.
I look—
this medieval visioner girl is kneeling
like St. Joan hands clasped so fervent
underneath her says, "chastity."

They're all talking telling stories
each one to beat another "hey me too,
I was starred special
I was graced by angels,"
that snatch hand   sort of thing

and beside them all a little boy was saying,
"Over here, over here
let's lift up the edge of this curtain
and go on in
to the pavilion"

and they did.

Because it meant falling
Because it meant finding a form.

Chapter XIX
Cross

I   Eyes

I

Will
> as the eye's abstract-more-beautiful-than-
> > sense

a suspension as makes flight
> be leaf
> fist-pushing porpoise
> upleaps.

Thus the academic meeting
> is a senseless
> marsh elder'd hour.

But when
> is duration felt?
> the dead who are already too given to what remains as touch
> they do not abide
> silently.

Under the hand of an eye a corridor is dreamt,
> but a sky's trailing fingers
> have already teased apart the walls.
> A harder will pushes out
> seed words scatter
> dandilion
> word carapace.

Among these
> what vanishing eye?

Taste is all in its deciding
> all touch rendered fruit,
> eye become word lies
> what fingers remember.

Body silt sifting last wine
> dregs death
> final taste-sign
> "gone fishin'."

As, not my will but hours passing
> a second de side
> haunt-parsed
> fingering pulse.

As others wade
> eye de-scripted
> where look has gone.

So love considers.

II

It was after a sill —
        eye spilled out memories as if
world was seen
        edgecup of beyond crossed

back and forth, hour after hour--
        nothing remains   of it;
without blood, an eye's milk waters less
        at last

whitepainted cherry under forgotten
        also passes with a body
night blurs into.

No more stars once
        that sill lip
Big Dipper   afterwards.

III

Eye's dam breaks and day floods out
        disappear stain soak in clay
or grass   deep black
        picture cards.

Floods ruin leaks desire Monet in kitchen tile
        leaks rivulet through love,
thumb flicker past past, part trees and houses
        spilled and lost

'till thirst wants more image
        'till the usual   at least
one glass,

    one more   glass of sunlight.

*****

deserveless
luck   done

*****

II   Stations or (Saturday Afternoon to Wonderland)

No work   but consumption   on no money —
tubercular windows of the Blue Line
and 37 views of Magic Mountain as ad flags along the window edge
out to Wonderland (dog race track)
a social act   in the sense of communion
on Saturday.

Other days the library is an option
but today Trinity goes past —
people in close spaces endure looks —
        an increasing onus is laid out by
the dead — all of us looking startled
and ashamed.

Yellow ceilings smell like piss
no one touches
in crowds climbing the stairs.

Overhead, a bare grass commons
despondent, unsupportable ideals—
"I had an abortion."

Change at government center's echoing vast
under the results of abstraction
these triangles and offices.

Blue line train tunnel,
Veronica's veil for sad eyes.

At aquarium
almost to Atlantic
lines of families
of the dead
in Easter hope
await tickets.

Above ground at
maverick,
a strange word
a place swept sea
immigrant women behind windows.
Airport is worse
the dead throng through
to the sea   to the sea.

What is left of raiment?
Cloud bank
train rattles past wood island.

Out to orient heights
which is to say Calvary tenements
at the Atlantic ledge.

Still among the slow dead
among the flocking
all of us,
and passion
those two.

We are somehow still alive
but ghost-lit
suffolk downs clatters by.

And then, as he is taken from the cross
as the crows scatter
the dunes of beachmont later.

A girl across looks out at the sea,
window cracked lets in brackish —
she shuts her eyes
until revere beach picnic shelters.

Its her stop
before the last
end of the line
at Wonderland.

III *Wrapped Shrouds*

I

Bees and new flies cloud the holly
despite roadwork; April sun much stronger
that should amaze   but's not there to pray.

You seek an old yew tree prescient as carshop shadows,
a Merlin salesman with Hegelian muscles,
sky reflected in used black Triumph.
Among the many possible rooms you had a ticket for
this one   which you held all the way here.

They say you walk off the path among trees
you'll see two trees like door posts
maybe one growing apart in a "V"
think: you step through you cross a threshold
you cross a threshold
that's prayer you step through
those two tree poems lifted
black stroke calligraphy
on the papery sky.
Then sometimes tickets and prayers don't match,
urban scape repeats when shuffled by morning —
you don't go through the sliding train windows
but slide too to the usual stop.

By St. John the Divine prayer is just brown bricks and
a less congested, more illustrated sky;
its bulk holds the city apart   like Moses
for a little while —

then the ticket-seller's return
tall masts of apartment buildings on every side
& gulls circle
the present.

*****

Then the great scaffold crow stoops
the tallest building's shadow.

*****

So perfect collaged
there's no edges

as seamless eye collapses   into display.

Such confusions are otherwise recognized
as what a room opens under certain passions
so vast a full world assumed

is dreamt.   This is the descant
perfect spider web   that hid Muhammad's cave
kiss of God,

and sometimes a girl   with secrets to tell

what passion means against the air —
          its full weight

once visited,
changes sky.

II

So often there is a threat an unseen
implication   your desire shares in —
It was happening again
you were running in a field
out across a field almost   free but
there were riders now
and so you fell   in the tall grass by a river —
there were cottonwoods
it was deep by the river and you turned
into a bird   and flew up
it was a good plan   you flew up and the riders
went by underneath
and it was Jesus   in armor and banners
and the horses   went down to the river
but because you were a bird
because transformation follows form   and birds soar and land
you lit in the grass again   you were naked in the grass
human   boy
and the horses were coming   back up
from the river.

III

She left a letter:
don't you understand?
Each of us kills
to live —
that's the threshold.

****

Fall, rise, fall
not waves or the sun
death so final   no metaphor
crosses
but crows gather sigil.

We rise to it too   each day
the light in our faces
half sun   but also this bright
endeavor

veils cannot conceal
nor color whisper lullaby to shelter
these long, fixed stares.

This life   all my beauty
each testimony I have sworn
each oath of loyal breath
as yours, O Earth
         I also die
despite   and orphan eyed.

Chapter XX
Touch My Side

I

A mosaic tile between fingers is not a word
      and yet is known by tracing it
with several touches
      or else is never known   because its not

a word;   even with eyes shut
      something is held   between;
in that way   world
      and body   take shape and skin

from a limit   a thousand limits   and apple branches —

but the invisible   said spirit aster   assonance
      as echo   whose tongue also kisses
presses back   what knowing

into body's ship?

II

If followed, the planets' design opens new folds
        an eye could trace
into the numberless grass sky,
        and even Descartes' grid makes knotted trails
towards unend   forever vectored axis   in spermy

idyll gyres:
        infinite distance   makes an answer
        we travel towards.

Limit without end
put your hand out
        and become   a further surface touched —

body becomes end-
        lessly

in love
        & thought follows sister after.

III

in the open, gravity untangles
its legs
like a colt

Part Four: Aftermath

Chapter XXI
Beside the Sea

I

It ended with the usual jealousies
someone fell off a ship
someone lay on another's breast
destinies were allotted
the teller won out
fish were laid out on coals
a beach grew dark
along the dunes, porch lights came on.

II

A tangle
our hearts
rose and briar
as
skin
is no limit
or castle

a tangle
Rose of Sharon sapling
asphalt nuance
in too many possible
readings.

III

Escape from desire when in it, but once outside nothing is as
sweet as becoming color again.

***

The lovers were fighting by the corner of the dairy isle
no, aisle
as inadequate canals
for what the sky feels
like.

****

The lovers fighting by the dairy aisle
were as beautiful
as God.

****

Because desire is God's rheostat
by which sensed *rooms*
become articulate.

****

Because desire is God's rheostat
by which sense becomes
articulate room.

IV

Desolate street signs—
raum and *niemand*—
as factory
not store

or
white stones in a sheep field

whisper, her shepherd.

****

In the room, birds flew more passionately
their vast armfuls
of fields.

****

Let the open roam through you O om,
home for this much vaster
silence.

V

Being established by lips,
        or tongue and teeth's hiss —
physical or essential,
        a body stakes difference   (tree

raised at the threshold
        a calligraphic lattice),   because
what's said is split be-
        tween you   and me —

wordliver that makes blood,
        broods through winter
dark, black glutinous slick

snailclump I spit the edges of
        mucusclot   you read back
suggested shore

transformed.

VI

Aspire essence caught by wet lungcloth surface
        phlegm and semen
mooncloud body leaking silvergrey raindrops
        and shadowwords, likeminnows
skim fast across pavement
        and grass.

Dense clustered bloodbag named
        "*piñata*" or Lot's wife pollen burst
taxonomical -ly -ly,
        your syllogistic fact.

Identity is *rendered* among displayed organs,
        is tabled aspiration sparsed—
"the sentence says"

"am" thunder "om"
        what lips press together
to kiss.

DAVID NEED has been a university lecturer in Asian Religions in Durham NC for twenty years. Book publications include two volumes of essays and translations on Rilke—Rainer Maria Rilke, *Roses: The Late French Poetry of Rainer Maria Rilke*, David Need, translations and essay, Horse and Buggy Press, 2014, and Rainer Maria Rilke, *Notebooks and Personal Papers*, David Need, translations and essays, Shearsman, 2018 — and one volume of his own poetry, *Offshore St, Mark / Songs in-Between the Day: Two Suites*, Three Count Pour, 2015. His poetry and critical writings have appeared in Hambone, Talisman, Golden Handcuffs Review, Lana Turner Review, Heavy Feathers Review, Spoke, Oyster Boy and Minor American.